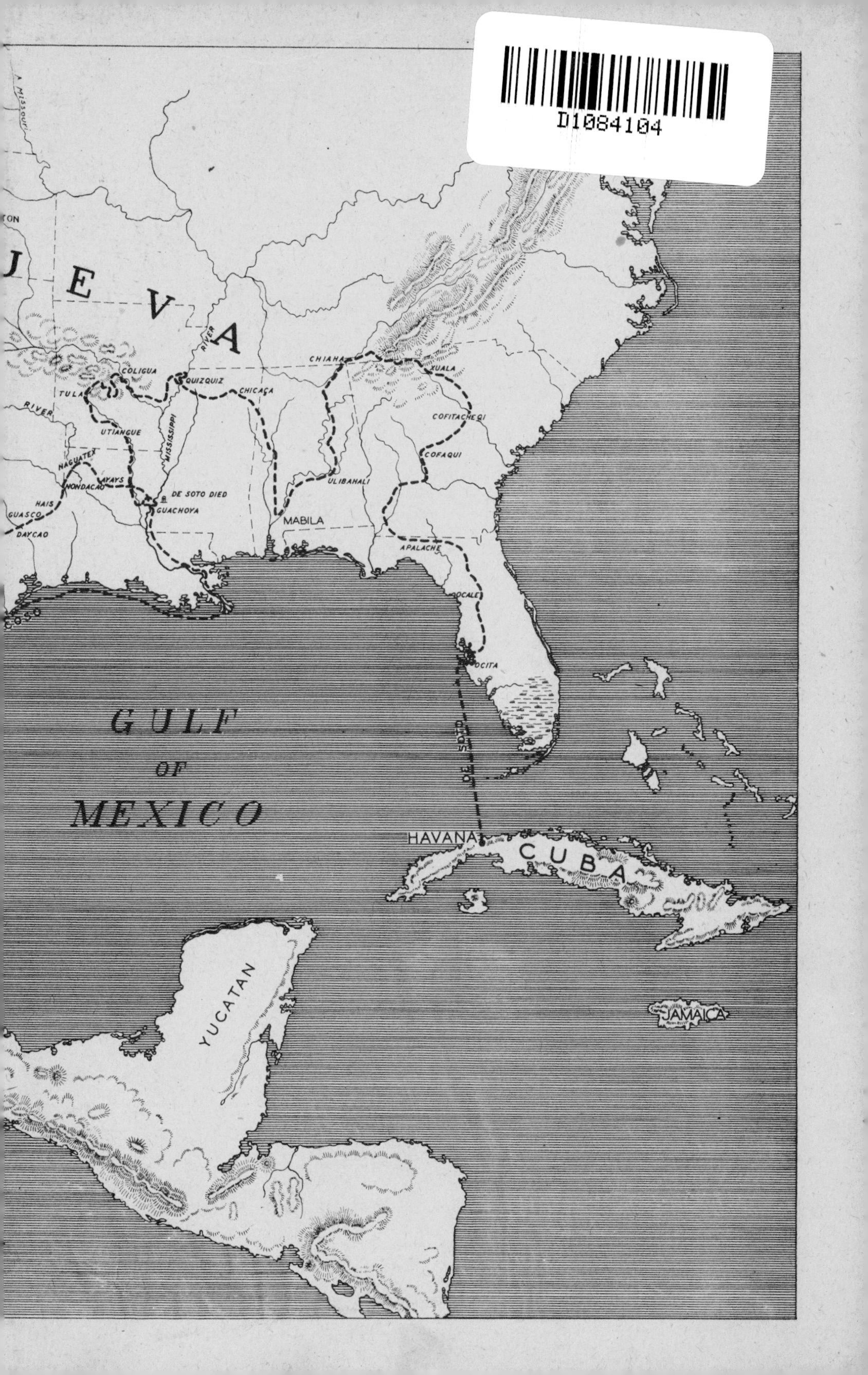

Missouri
J E V A
RIVER
COLIGUA
QUIZQUIZ
TULA
RIVER
CHICAÇA
CHIAHA
XUALA
UTIANGUE
MISSISSIPPI
COFITACHEQI
COFAQUI
NAGUATEX
AYAYS
NONDACAO
ULIBAHALI
DE SOTO DIED
HAIS
GUACHOYA
GUASCO
DAYCAO
MABILA
APALACHE
COSO
OCALE
OCITA
GULF
OF
MEXICO
DE SOTO
HAVANA
CUBA
YUCATAN
JAMAICA

C O R O N A D O

KNIGHT OF PUEBLOS AND PLAINS

CORONADO

KNIGHT OF PUEBLOS AND PLAINS

By Herbert E. Bolton

WHITTLESEY HOUSE
McGraw-Hill Book Company, Inc.—New York, London, Toronto
AND
THE UNIVERSITY OF NEW MEXICO PRESS
Albuquerque, New Mexico

CORONADO

Published by Whittlesey House
A division of the McGraw-Hill Book Company, Inc.
and
The University of New Mexico Press

Printed in the United States of America
American Book–Stratford Press, Inc., New York

Dedicated to all my good companions on the trail and to my many students who vicariously have accompanied me in my ramblings

PREFACE

This book starts off with a conscious falsification, not even calling the principal character by his right name. Arciniegas, in his delightful volume called *The Knight of El Dorado,* confesses to the same crime and explains how it happened. "Throughout the whole conquest of America one never knows who is who. Names are always being changed about. . . . Sebastián de Belalcázar, for example, was named Sebastián Moyano, but historians wrote reams of paper, saying, some, that he was called Belalcázar, and others, Benalcázar. As a matter of fact, he was probably not a Moyano at all but a García. Let the reader go to Quito, Popayán, or Cali, however, and tell residents that the founder of their city was named García Moyano, and they will laugh in his face, if they do not stone him to death." In the same way, the famous pioneer of Arizona, New Mexico, Texas, Oklahoma, and Kansas was Francisco Vázquez de Coronado, but few persons now living in these regions would recognize him under his correct name of Vázquez, and they might assassinate a writer who should insist on being accurate on that point. Not wishing the crown of martyrdom, even for the sake of veracity, I shall conform to well established custom and call him Coronado. The case is similar with García López de Cárdenas, Coronado's ablest lieutenant and discoverer of Grand Canyon. By his contemporaries he was called López, but in this gringo country he is known as Cárdenas, and so he is designated here.

To catch the significance of Coronado he must be seen in perspective. In 1848 gold was discovered at Sutter's Mill in California. The news got out, and within a year fifty thousand Argonauts from all parts of the world found their way to the Promised Land, hoping to make their fortunes, go back home, and live happily ever afterward. In the mines not one in a thousand struck it rich, and the rank and file scarcely averaged a dollar a day for their toil. The California Gold Rush was a typical episode which had been repeated innumerable times in America since Columbus' celebrated voyage. In essence it was not greatly different from the remarkable treasure hunts which swept over a large part of the Western Hemisphere in the second quarter of the sixteenth century. We justly glorify our Forty-niners, but we have customarily applied the term "wild-goose chases" to earlier quests for the Golden Fleece. One of these was the Coronado Expedition, whose four hundredth anniversary we have recently commemorated.

Set in motion by a story not altogether unlike that of Marshall's discovery in California, Coronado and his followers made known the great Southwest and contributed toward its permanent settlement. Leaving Mexico City in 1540 with some three hundred Spaniards and a large body of Indian allies, Don Francisco went west to the Pacific Ocean, ascended the coast through the regions now known as Sinaloa and Sonora, explored Arizona and New Mexico, marched out upon the buffalo-covered plains of Texas, discovered Tule and Palo Duro canyons, turned north through Oklahoma, entered Kansas, reached the Arkansas River near the site of Ford (so designated for the historic crossing there), and followed the stream to Quivira, a name then given to the Wichita Indian settlements between the Arkansas and Smoky Hill rivers. Meanwhile Alarcón with part of Coronado's force ascended the Gulf of California and explored the lower Colorado River. Incidentally, he reached California two years ahead of Cabrillo, the reputed discoverer.

First among Europeans, Coronado and his men saw and described on the basis of eye-witness information the Zuñi Pueblos, the Hopi Pueblos, Colorado River, Grand Canyon, Gila River, and the giant Yuman tribes along the River of the Firebrands. Farther east they were first to see Ácoma, "the Sky City," the upper Rio Grande, the Tiguex Pueblos along its banks, snow-covered Sangre de Cristo Mountains, Pecos River, Canadian River, the vast herds of buffaloes, and the great canyons of the Staked Plains, as later they were miscalled by the Anglo-American pioneers. They first explored the Texas Panhandle, first crossed Oklahoma, the Cimarron and Arkansas rivers, traversed eastern Kansas, and became acquainted with the tattooed Wichitas. These helmet-crested Spanish horsemen saw and made known to the world most of the places visited today by myriad travelers in the region now known in the United States as the Far Southwest.

Coronado thus performed in North America a feat of adventure and discovery comparable to what was done in South America in the same period by Pizarro, Almagro, Belalcázar, or Quesada, and in Middle America by Cortés, Guzmán, or Alvarado. He converted the old trail up the West Coast Corridor of Mexico into a well-known road which is still in use as an automobile highway and as the route of the Southern Pacific Railroad. Historical tradition in the vast area up the Corridor, and all the way from California to Kansas, runs back four centuries to the spectacular expedition made by Don Francisco and his companions.

The impress left by the young Spaniard on the history and lore of the Southwest is patent and still growing. Geographical designations given or first made known to Europeans by Don Francisco and his men are found all over the map. Names reminiscent of his adventure have been assigned to a multitude of places, objects, institutions, and organizations. We find among Arizona place names Alarcón Terrace, Cárdenas Butte, Coronado Park, Conquistador Aisle, Coronado International Memorial Park, Coronado Mesa, Coronado Mountains, Coronado Summit, Coronado Trail (U. S. Highway No. 666), El Despoblado, Fray Marcos Mountain, Padilla Mesa, Tovar Mesa, and Tobar Terrace. In New Mexico, besides the names of many Indian pueblos first made known by Coronado, there are Cíbola National Forest, Coronado State Monument, and Gran Quivira National Monument. In Kansas we encounter Eldorado and Coronado Heights. Coronado City and Coronado Beach in California, it may be noted, get their names not from Coronado the explorer, but from nearby islands whose designation alludes to certain Christian martyrs. Besides geographical names commemorating Coronado's exploit, the Southwest has Coronado motor courts, schools, and theaters, and at least one Coronado cattle ranch. There is a Coronado hotel as far east as Philadelphia. Among commercial and industrial enterprises one finds a Coronado Carbon Company, a Coronado Petroleum Company, and a Coronado Exploration Company, whose business is that of prospecting for oil.

Somewhat more highbrow than any of the foregoing memorials to the explorer is the historical organization called the Quivira Society. In Omaha even the *bon ton* bow to the famous general. There a leading social group styled Ak-Sar-Ben each year commemorates the Coronado Expedition to Quivira, in whose tradition Nebraska claims a share. In 1940 several of the Southwestern states conducted Coronado celebrations in honor of the four hundredth anniversary of the expedition, conspicuous among them being the one held in New Mexico. The legislature of that commonwealth formed a Coronado Cuarto Centennial Commission which carried out an elaborate and state-wide celebration. As a part of the Coronado memorial the University of New Mexico is issuing a series of historical volumes called the Coronado Cuarto Centennial Publications.

The Coronado Expedition shares in the tradition of Mexico as well as of the United States. Don Francisco Vázquez de Coronado was a conspicuous and honored figure at the court of Mendoza, first viceroy of New Spain. His wife, Doña Beatríz de Estrada, was the wealthiest heiress in the Mexico of her day, notable for her piety and charity, and her fame is recorded on her tomb in one of North America's most historic churches. As governor of Nueva Galicia, which then embraced a vast area west of the capital,

Coronado occupies many pages in the annals of Guadalajara, Compostela, Tepic, and Culiacán, those old cities which charm every visitor within their gates. His spectacular expedition is a chapter in the history of the Mexican states of Jalisco, Nayarit, Sinaloa, and Sonora, as well as of our great Southwest. Thus he is an immortal link between the republics of Mexico and the United States. To symbolize this early historic bond the governments of Mexico and the United States have plans for setting aside and developing an area on the Sonora-Arizona boundary line as a Coronado International Monument.

Whatever merit may be claimed for this book must be left to others than myself. But it may be appropriate to say that besides consulting extensive manuscript sources that hitherto have been used little or not at all, I have made a more detailed reconnoissance of Coronado's route of travel and the scenes of his adventure than any of my predecessors, and thereby have been able to vivify the episode, to clear up many obscure or disputed points, and to offer new interpretations.

TABLE OF CONTENTS

CHAPTER I

EL DORADO

The Spanish occupation of mainland America proceeded from an already established base in the West Indies, where Columbus had planted the first European colony in America. Grijalva, sent out to explore by the governor of Cuba, gathered gold on the coast of Mexico and heard of the rich Aztec civilization in the interior. Thereupon Hernando Cortés, with some five hundred men, thirty muskets, a few toy cannons, and sixteen horses, set forth in 1519 from Cuba, a rebel against the island governor, to conquer this land of rumored gold. He arrived on the Vera Cruz coast with sixteen horses and a colt. Here, Grijalva's report was confirmed by the lavish present sent to the bold invader by Montezuma, the frightened ruler at the Aztec capital situated on a lake on the high plateau 250 miles inland.

This astonishing gift was emphatic evidence of the great wealth of Mexico. The present included a gold necklace set with emeralds and hung with pearls, a huge golden disk, as large as a wagon wheel, representing the sun, and another of silver to simulate the moon. There were gold and silver ornaments and toys, feather headdresses decorated with gems, pearl-pointed tridents, amazing feather-work, garments of finely woven cotton, and what were called "books" written in hieroglyphics. The bare list of items comprised in the gift occupies several pages of modern print. It was one of the decisive documents in world history, for it caused a "gold rush" embracing two-thirds of the hemisphere, and brought about revolutionary changes in America, Europe, and Asia.

Montezuma had sent these lavish offerings to induce the unwelcome visitor to depart, but they merely whetted his appetite and fired his imagination. Don Hernando, in turn, sent the treasure to Spain as a bribe to soften the heart of Charles V toward a rebel, and then marched boldly toward the Aztec capital, fighting battles and winning native allies as he went. In spite of a veritable "Dunkirk" in the Noche Triste retreat, he overthrew Montezuma, made himself master of the heart of the country, was forgiven for rebellion, and rewarded by being made captain-general and marquis, with thousands of tributary subjects.

Cortés, by his lucky strike, set everybody in motion. To discover other Mexicos, great prospecting expeditions were organized, some launched in Spain, some in the islands, and others on the mainland of North and South America. As a rule they were privately financed, for the Emperor was thrifty. A typical expedition consisted of a few hundred Spaniards, followed by hordes of natives carrying the baggage, opening roads, performing camp duty, and serving as couriers and interpreters. As far as possible the invaders lived off the country they raided. But in most cases, as a precautionary measure, a commissary department was driven on all fours, and included droves of hogs, herds of cattle, and flocks of sheep and goats, brought from Spain or the West Indies with immeasurable difficulty. Supply ships crossing the ocean with livestock and provisions stank to heaven. Below the Isthmus of Panama, immense droves of llamas were taken along both as pack animals and to serve as food. An airplane view of *Mundus Novus* at almost any time in the two decades after 1520 would have disclosed several different bands of these gold-thirsty prospectors, crawling like armies of ants across the face of the Hemisphere in numerous regions wide apart, all bound on the same errand. In some instances they were able to penetrate the mainland by the great river systems. But whether they traveled by water or by land, their object was the same—wealth and adventure. The ranks of these armies were filled with eager young fellows who had read in Spain or obtained in the book stalls of Mexico and Lima the romances of chivalry just then being published—*Amadís de Gaula, Las Serges de Esplandián, Palmería de Oliva,* and a dozen others, whose influence in the conquest Dr. Irving Leonard has so convincingly set forth.

Many individual soldiers of fortune were ubiquitous, appearing, in spite of the difficulties of travel, here, there, and yonder, now at the top and then at the bottom of the map, like the proverbial prospector who joins every new gold rush. The names of some of these repeaters are familiar to every schoolboy. De Soto pioneered in regions as far apart as Central America, Peru, Florida, and the Mississippi Valley; Pedro de Alvarado in Mexico, Central America, and Ecuador; Cabeza de Vaca in Texas, Mexico, and Paraguay. Las Casas was with the vanguard in Guatemala, Peru, and Mexico; Fray Juan de Padilla in Tehuantepec, Jalisco, New Mexico, and Kansas.

On the mainland the regions inhabited by sedentary natives were usually first to be subjugated, and they became the first centers of permanent Spanish settlement on a considerable scale. The reasons for this are not far to seek. Sedentary people were the easiest to conquer, for they had fixed homes and could not run away. They were the most worth exploiting because they were accustomed to disciplined labor. They had a steady food supply and, in some cases, an accumulation of precious metals. Their daughters were pleasing, so there were many thousands of "Pocahontases" in America long before the days of John Smith of Jamestown. When the Europeans entered the interior they carried with them the extravagant tales they had heard in Europe or the islands, added to their repertoire new ones gathered on the way, and embroidered them with fantastic passementerie of their own fabrication, sometimes with waggish humor. Each track made by the explorers on the enormous map of the New World represents some glowing idea, some feverish quest, and effort to run to its source this or that tale of treasure, some rumored city, some wonder in the country beyond—*mas allá*.

In this expansion the lieutenants of Cortés quickly extended their conquests in all directions from the Aztec capital till most of the sedentary peoples of central and southern Mexico were under Spanish control. Red-headed Pedro de Alvarado pushed into Guatemala, seat of an old civilization, in some respects more remarkable than that of the Aztecs. Panama became a base for expeditions northward into Central America which met and contested the field with the men of Cortés. The fever spread to South America. Panama City was barely three years old when adventurers began to sail down the Pacific coast to investigate rumors of great wealth in Peru. Francisco Pizarro, cousin of Cortés, set forth from the Isthmus to emulate his now millionaire relative. Like Mexico, Peru was easy to conquer because of internal dissensions. Atahualpa, governor of Quito, was in rebellion against the Inca at Cuzco. Pizarro marched inland over the towering Andes and captured Atahualpa, who for his ransom paid a room full of gold and another of silver, the combined value of which has been estimated at several millions of dollars. Pizarro now made himself master of a large part of Peru, founded Lima, and extended his conquest into what are now Bolivia and Chile. Thus Mexico and Lima, established by two humble cousins from rock-strewn Estremadura in Mother Spain, became the capitals of Spanish North and South America.

Settlers at Santa Marta, near the mouth of the great Magdalena River, which pours its waters northward into the Caribbean Sea, heard the legend of the Gilded Man. It told of a tribe in the south, on the high plateau of Bogotá, whose chief was installed by an unusual rite of deep religious significance. He was anointed with oil and sprinkled with gold dust, then, being pushed on a raft out upon the sacred lake of Guatavitá, he dived into the water and washed off the gleaming metal. As part of the ceremony the natives threw into the lake countless gold ornaments and precious stones as offerings to the gods. The gold-sprinkled chief became known to the Spaniards as El Dorado—the Gilded Man. This story inspired a new series of epic marches southward from the Spanish Main, a three-cornered struggle among conquerors, and the founding, by Quesada, of the city of Bogotá, now the cultured capital of the Republic of Colombia. The longest chase of El Dorado was still to come, for when Quesada reached Guatavitá, the Gilded Man was no longer there, so the treasure hunters continued the search eastward over the Andes. In the quest, Orellano navigated the largest river in the world to its mouth. Because of a battle with brawny women on its banks, so the story goes, the river was called and still is known as the Amazon. All this had happened within the space of a few years.

The military success of these small bands of Spaniards—a few hundred in each army at the most—was due to the ability and boldness of their leaders, their possession of gunpowder and horses, and the lack of organization and equipment of the natives. Indians using bows and arrows were as helpless in the face of mounted men and fire-arms as were some of the armies of World War II which, using the weapons of 1914, had to oppose modern tanks and bombing planes. Even more important than the material equipment of the Europeans were the hordes of native allies who joined the invaders. In fact, it might well be said that the Spaniards did not conquer America—the natives, led by the Spaniards, conquered each other.

Cortés, meanwhile, had been active in western Mexico, seeking other El Dorados. He extended the conquest across Michoacán, and, less than a year after the fall of the Aztec capital, his lieutenants reached the Pacific Ocean and there established bases for expansion by sea. A ship sent by Cortés from Zacatula in 1527, safely reached the Moluccas, thus making the first American voyage to the Orient—two and one-half centuries ahead of Robert Gray. Colima, founded on the coast at the foot of the towering volcano, became a base for long strides up the map in pursuit of new and old objectives. The search for slaves, gold, and silver led in that direction. Other lures were reports of a good harbor and tales of Amazons. Native chiefs, said Cortés, "affirm that there is an island inhabited only by women . . . and that at certain times men from the mainland visit them." So the excitement increased.

The conqueror of Mexico was now summoned to Spain to defend his rights in America, and the advance up the west coast was continued by his tough-fibered rival, Nuño de Guzmán.

In 1529 Don Nuño left central Mexico with five hundred Spaniards and several thousand native allies. At Tepic he established a garrison, the germ of the capital of the present state of Nayarit. Going north, and failing to find the Amazons, he turned his attention to a search for the legendary Seven Cities, long famed in European tradition and now transplanted to America. Some time previously, when a conquistador in Pánuco, Don Nuño had contemplated an expedition to the northern interior. An Indian named Tejo told him of a trading jaunt which he had once made with his father in that direction to some rich and populous cities, seven in number. Like the story of the Amazons, this one of Seven Cities came out of the distant past and was brought to America by the discoverers. In the Middle Ages, so the old tale ran, seven Portuguese bishops, pressed by the conquering Mohammedans, fled west into the "Ocean Sea," and founded the Seven Cities of Antilia—hence the name Antilles, given by the Spaniards to the West Indian islands. The story was not confined to Portuguese and Spanish circles. John Cabot, after his celebrated voyage to Newfoundland in 1497 in the service of England, was reputed to have discovered "the isles of Brazil and the Seven Cities," as well as the Kingdom of the Gran Khan of China. Now, if Tejo told the truth, seven cities had been visited not long ago by natives of Mexico. Could these be the same as those of the legend? Whatever they might be, Guzmán decided to seek them by crossing the formidable Sierra Madre Occidental, for it was from Pánuco in the east that Tejo had journeyed north with his father to those terraced towns. The difficult march was made in vain; but, to secure the lands he had conquered on the west coast, Guzmán established the permanent settlement of Culiacán in 1531, just a century before the founding of Boston. Don Nuño himself now withdrew to Tepic, but his colonists extended their explorations and slave hunting raids as far north as the Yaqui River.

This advance into Sinaloa and Sonora by land spurred Cortés to further activities by sea. Returning to Mexico he renewed his expeditions up the coast. Four years later Jiménez, one of his sea captains, discovered pearls on the Peninsula of California,